AF264345

This book is dedicated to the little Black girl
who is sometimes tricked into feeling like she
isn't enough and may even be teased by
others her age.

I pray that it helps you see that you are more
than enough the way God created you.

BEAUTIFUL
Just As I Am
(daily positive affirmations for Black girls)

Illustrated By:
Cheryl Tyson

Written By:
Justine Disasi

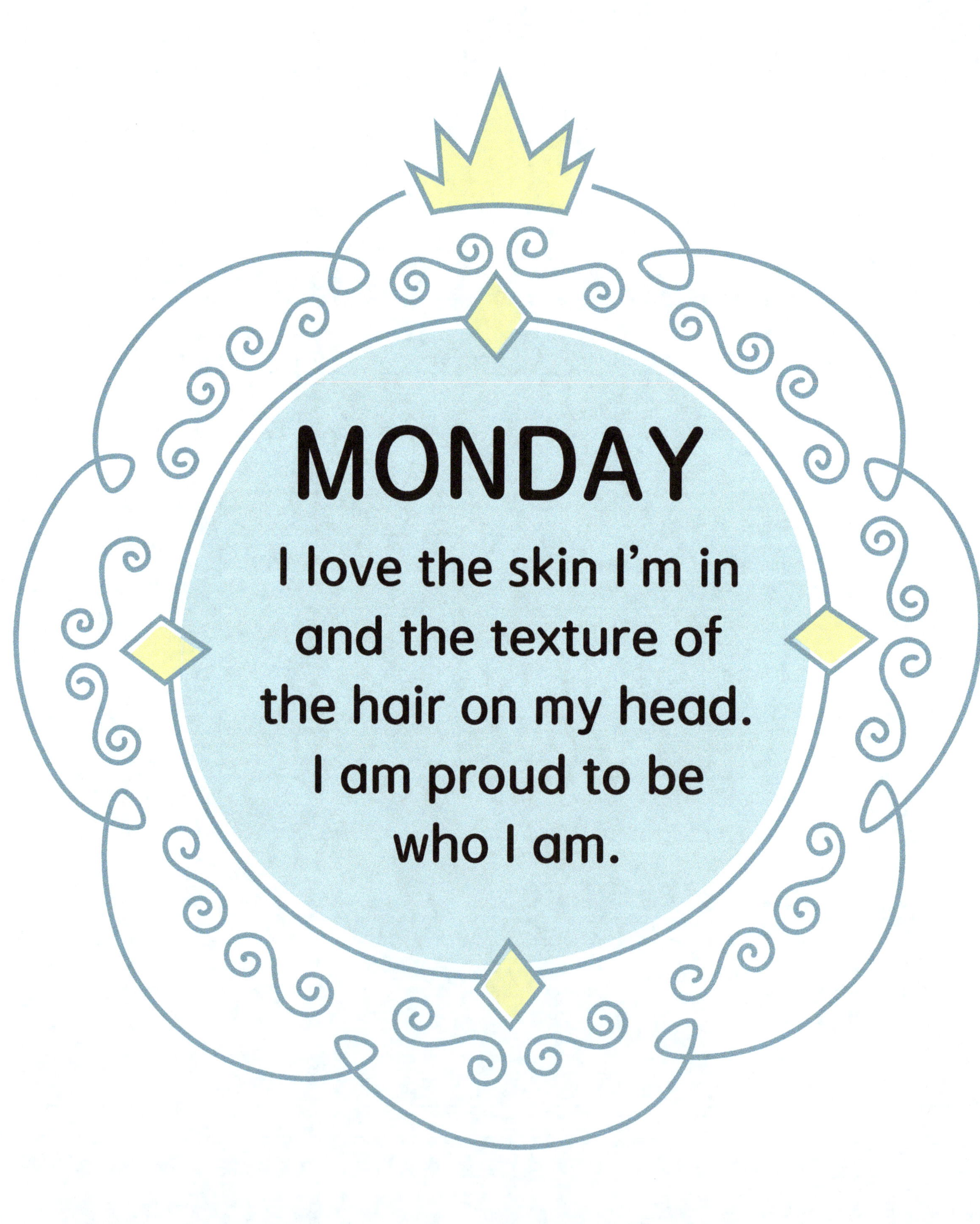
MONDAY
I love the skin I'm in
and the texture of
the hair on my head.
I am proud to be
who I am.

TUESDAY
I can accomplish anything I put my mind to do. I am unstoppable.
The sky is the limit.

WEDNESDAY
I am beautiful no
matter what I wear.
I am creative and I
will change the
world around me.

THURSDAY
I am strong and can conquer anything.
I am fearless and full of potential.
My bald is beautiful.

FRIDAY
I am grateful for my
body and all bodies
are beautiful.
I get to enjoy this
world and create
fun memories.

BE KIND

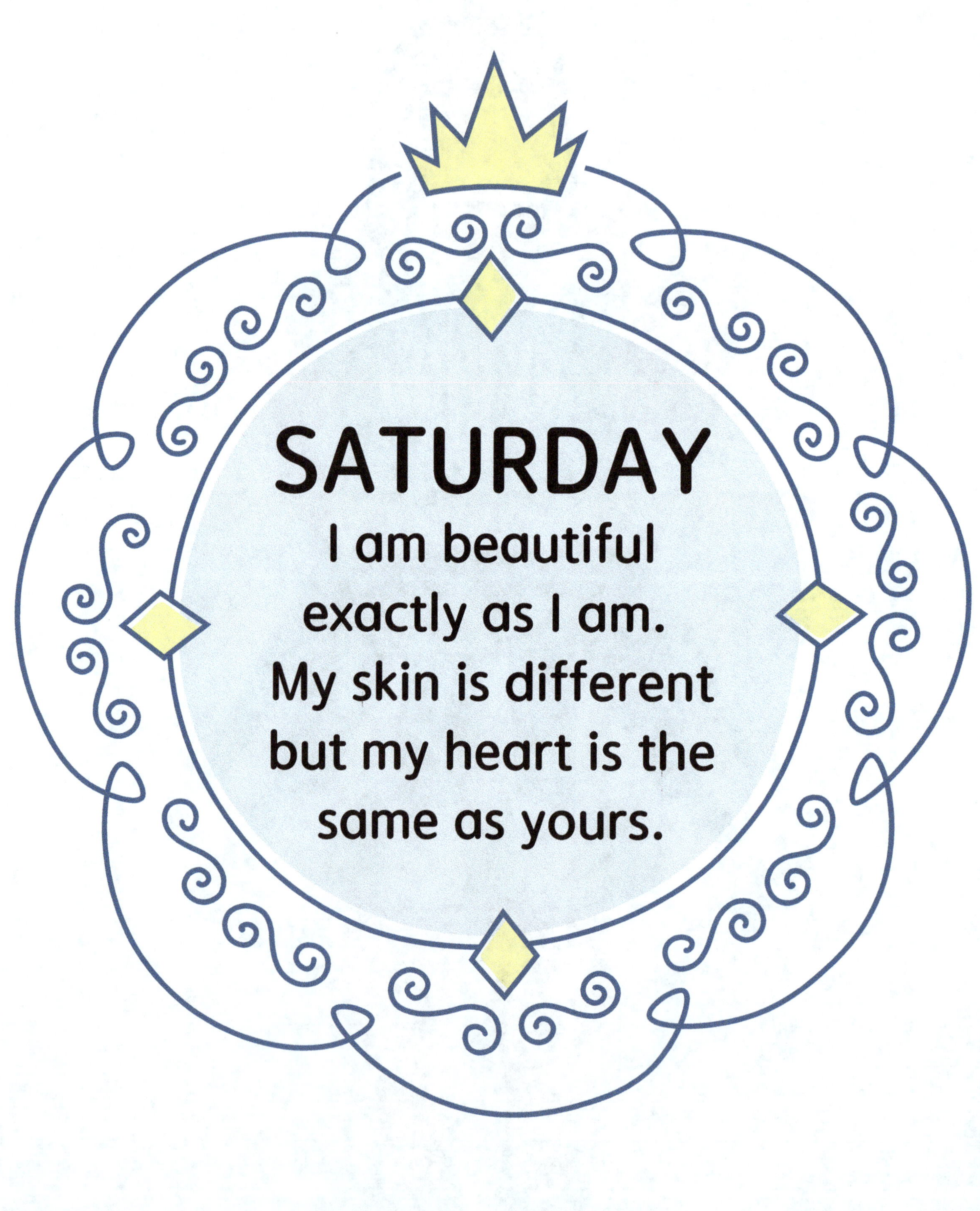
SATURDAY
I am beautiful
exactly as I am.
My skin is different
but my heart is the
same as yours.

SUNDAY
The love my family
has for me is
enough.
I always have
someone rooting
for me.

I AM:
Fearless
Beautiful
Unstoppable
Creative
Strong
Fearfully and
wonderfully made

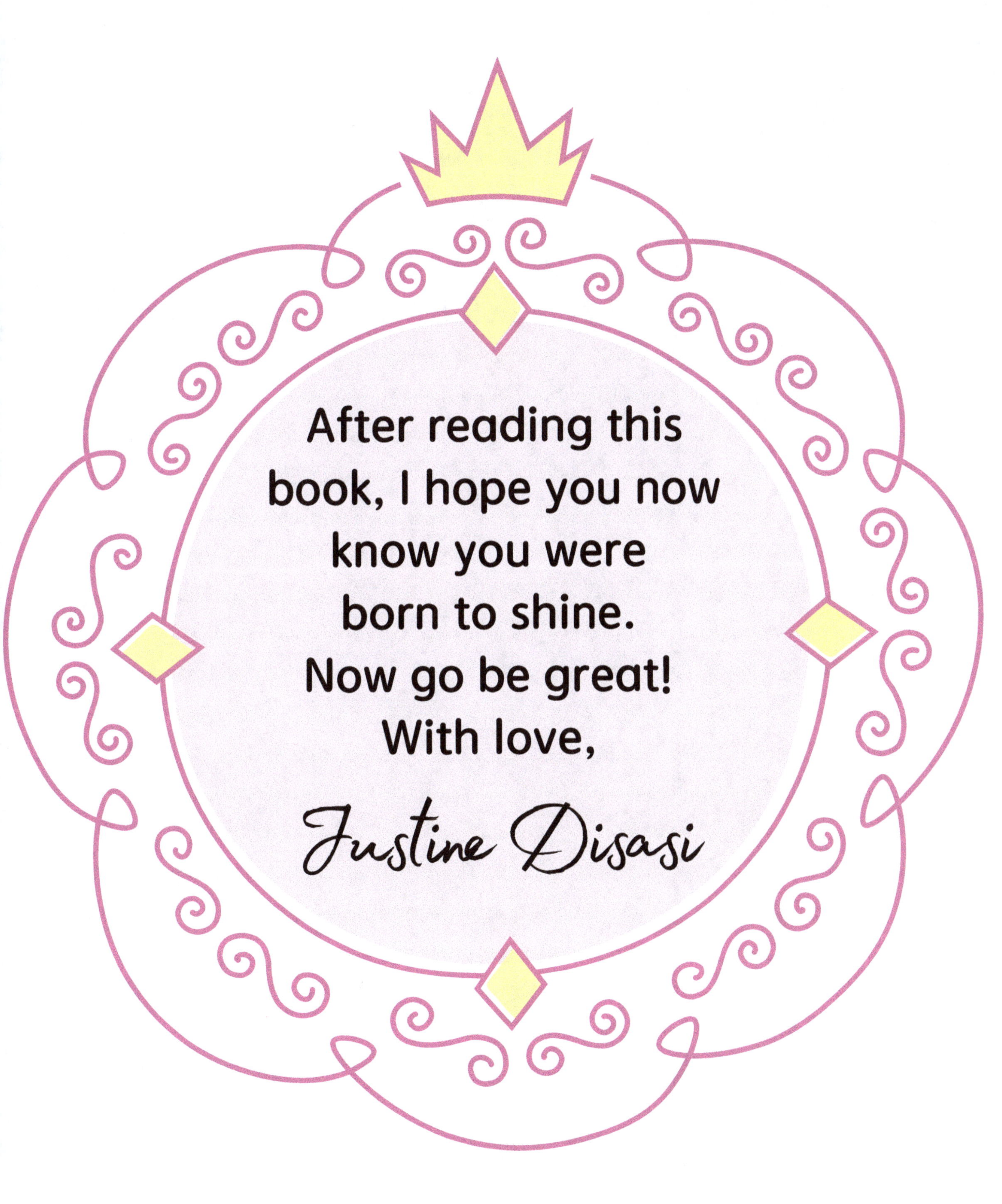

After reading this
book, I hope you now
know you were
born to shine.
Now go be great!
With love,

Justine Disasi